MAGPIES IN THE VALLEY OF OLEANDERS

Also by Author

You Are Indeed an Elk, But This is Not the Forest You Were Born to Graze
Gold Wake, 2014

Magpies in the Valley of Oleanders

Poems by Kyle McCord

Copyright © Kyle McCord 2016

No part of this book may be used or performed without written consent from the author, if living, except for critical articles or reviews.

McCord, Kyle
1st edition.

ISBN: 978-0-9965864-2-9
Library of Congress Control Number: 2015915111

Interior Layout by Lea C. Deschenes
Cover Design by Dorinda Wegener
Cover Art: "View of the Arco Valley in the Tyrol" by Albrecht Dürer, ca. 1495
    WikiArt.org & Wikipaintings.org: Public Domain, U.S. Copyright Law
    File Source: www.the-athenaeum.org
Editing by Matt Mauch and Tayve Neese

Printed in Tennessee, USA
Trio House Press, Inc.
Ponte Vedra Beach, FL

To contact the author, send an email to tayveneese@comcast.net

TABLE OF CONTENTS

I.

3	Lesser Evil
6	Gentle
8	Portrait of Vincent in Nuenen
11	Aubade for the World in Miniature
14	Triptych for Nighthawks
17	How to Fall in Love with the Prairie
21	Self-Portrait at Twenty-Eight in Iberia
23	Poem with Sky Cradled in Shrunken Limbs
26	First Course in Demonology
29	August 5, 2012
32	Triptych with Burning Branches (Refrain)
34	Elegy for the Deodand

II.

39	Disciplining the Body
42	Self-Portrait of Daughter as Eurydice
44	A Prayer for Anesthetics and Illusion
46	On Dignity
48	Self-Portrait of Rossetti Among the Dead

50	Burning and Getting Burnt
52	Pentimento
55	Soviet Film
57	Self-Portrait as Hunters in the Snow
60	Dürer in the Valley of Oleanders
62	Politics of the Afterlife
65	Three Trees for Lydia
69	Acknowledgments
71	About the Author

I.

Lesser Evil

Museum of the Occupation of Latvia, 2012

In the display case
  rills of script fill the open ledgers—
    Liga, Dzintra, Janis,
    Oskar, Sandra—

a codex for the Nazis' victims,
  tome after tome for Stalin's.

Tap your hand lightly
  against the opaque

as though some knuckle
  branded by frostbite
    might echo,

a phantom the boxcars
  ferried from
    Yuhnov or Vyatka.

Let their names
  slick your lips—

names which could mean
  what to you?

Syllables pulled from survivors
  sure and cold as a projector
    gumming film.

Imagine choosing
    between two butchers,
        your brother's murderer
        or your other brother's murderer.

Your tour huddles
    around a steel terminal,

the great leader
    in his admiral's cap.

Consider
    his Georgian brow—
    stern, confident

or the toddler who returns
    his gaze, mouths a slur
        of vowels.

Many Latvians greeted
    the Nazis, a tour guide adds,

at least they killed
    more discriminately.

Behind her, a lithograph:

the limp bodies of nationalists,
    hung from
    a fruit stand.

Here, you think, it's always
    one evil you know
    then another.

Imagine the cobbled square
   beyond these walls,
      the onyx stallions
         lining its rooftops.

Your choices now are simple:
   celebrate this statuary
   under hunger moon,
   or mourn the dead.

Is it a choice?

Before you: a violin
    molded from soup bones,
    strung with horse hair.

Will you play it tonight,
   wanderer, and
      if so, for whom?

Gentle

Driving Bill to the airport,
he pointed out the window.
Cormorant, he said. And I turned
long enough to catch a glimpse—
the bird
above a smokestack,
above the discount mattress store,

where I've never seen a single car.
The sky's auburn star
flared russet on its back.

It was beautiful, Lydia,
the bird,
but also the way he named it,
like he couldn't hold the word's weight
once he'd spotted it.

Only a night since Bill
opened his book
in the bar haunted by smoke
to read about his daughter.
Uhte, he said, *unheimlich*.

And later asked
could one of the dogs stay
with him, the corgi
named for a lover of nightingales.

He's a man who knows his bedfellows.

I'm an oar held
in streams of dawn.

Now only 8 a.m., and the stars
already cleared, my hands
newly anemic.

To crave
language
is to love another thing,
my friend, not the many faces
I can no longer conjure.

Sweet one not you
eyeing a curler
as it coils you to helix.

I watched you naked
before the mirror—
what word
a match for you.
*My amaretto. My star-
bitten bird.*

I think again of how
Bill removed his glasses,
rubbed his eyes.
Magpies, how amazing,
he pointed,
and meant the bird—
or, tell me,
could he mean the word
it slowly became?

Portrait of Vincent in Nuenen

After The Potato Eaters, *1885*

Isn't he happy here,
easel set toward the cottage,
bank of bluing clouds
scalded at their brink?
No boys hocking nests today,
no Margot lounging on the lawn.

Yes, it might have been pleasant
to trace roosts of her hair,
taut skin of her brow
serious
    as he is young.
But instead hours
are mustard, dun,
dark mahogany
for varicose branchlets.

DeGroot's wife
is a *Levenslied*, a life-song,
as she shuffles
candle to candle
in the windows of the hut.

He watches her
fill them with wisps,
watches her wash floors in ember.

He'd like to paint fire,
smolder;
    the hut as flame
floods everything.

But how to detail ruin?
Its strokes unlike
the paced work of seasons,
the wrinkles lengthening
DeGroot's gravedigger's hands.

They remind him of roans
he watched last spring,
how their dark hides matted
with exhaustion.

How their bones shook
beneath a thunder
of muscles,
    an elegance
so hideous it made him sick.

How could he amputate
those manes feathered
against gaunt snow?
How to paint beauty
that heedless?

To them, he's another beast
howling
    to a second sky.

A shade turning in for tubers,
black tea.

Hard to tell wife from daughter,
hard too
    to tell workhorses
from roans scattering
poppies.

Left to their incivility,
they'd swallow potatoes whole.

Surely,
    they'd snap the wind's neck.

Aubade for the World in Miniature

After Katrin Sigurdardottir's Haul, *2005*

The broadleaf and birch
    rendered in polymer
        darken
            below
                plaster Fjällen,

unpeopled alpines,
    which bound
        Sigurdardottir's
            Swedish wilderness.

The docent shows me cam locks,
    hinges that fold the landscape

        turn fjords
            to clouds,
        meadowland
            to verdigris bulwarks.

They arrive just like that, he says.

No cottages
    and no smoke
        of ashen flower-wire,

just permafrosted expanses
    and the Ljungan—

      the dreadful in Old Norse—
          twisting off
                into nothing.

Look in my eyes,
    and you'll see a man in love
        with the miniature.

I want to sleep
    on the moon
        of that ice cap.
            Smoke
a pipe in the river's
    shallows.

Come, be my house god,
    I want to say.

In the rose garden,
    walk with me where ice dies
        on the stone monoliths,
            muscular arenite eggs.

Those cairns so disproportionate,
    the cherry plum,
        what must be the caretaker's house

        beyond.

Run your hand
    along the sculpture's bulk.

Aren't the cirri riders,
    their detritus wispy hooves?

Couldn't we be one being
    at so great a distance?

Everything below
   pale,
   indistinct.

Why refuse
   this world
   our music, beautiful,

all we have?

Triptych for Nighthawks

It feels strange to happen upon them
in the heat of Texas:

the man in the pewter fedora,
the broad-shouldered redhead.

Her nearly shuttered lids
betray a distance

as tangible
as the cherry wood counters.

There's something about the boy
I've never liked: how he seems

caught in his own innocence,
an unwitting extra,

whose expression
may as well be a *momento mori*,

the last grimace of the moth
yearning toward the bulb.

My father hung the print in his office,
an ironic homage to Hemingway's killers

perched above the rows
of leather-bound law reviews.

But a venous seam divided the diner.
A range of wrinkles topographically

spreading along the stranger
isolated enough to worry.

Hours waiting in his office,
I'd unfocus my eyes and let

blemish blur the scene into diptych—
the diner on one side

and the sfumato corner where some
shadow lurked on the other.

Easy for vision to divide,
but if art can fashion

the foreign to the familiar,
how can it be trusted? I wondered.

I encountered the painting
again at a party in Aarhus.

The night before
lightning had stitched ash

along the invasive hedge maple
between a doctor's house

and mine.
When she grabbed my hand,

I was glad to leave
the tree's chiaroscuro shadow,

how its blackened teeth
turned inward on themselves.

She slurred words
as she pointed to the print.

Only the corymbs flowering
my father's canvas were absent.

A little bit of home, she said
and leaned in to kiss me,

her lips as familiar and alien
as the painting itself.

In the gallery, the clouds
turned the color of turmeric.

*Have you witnessed the sun
set in our country?* she asked

relishing what novelty
she could lay before me—

the martini blue garments
and the yard's unset bone

horribly charred
and holding up the sky.

How to Fall in Love
with the Prairie

After Courbet's The Cliff at Etretat after the Storm, *1869*

In the meth dealer's farmhouse,
    the windows glow like lanterns.

No tiki torches,
    no comforting smoke,

only a barn light
    blinks
    and crackles.

In the farmhouse,
    daughters barter
    breaths of sleep.

Their mason jar of fireflies
    emits distress,

but better you rejoin the path
    past the witch hazels

and trumpet creepers.

Better not to wander
    this robber's highway,

which would lead you where?

Another acreage,
another parsonage
    resident
      to elements.

You can stay if you like.
    Run-off mimes
        the play of phantoms,

plinking,
    bumping
    the rotten paneling.

In the expanse beyond the ridge
    could be anything, really,

even Courbet's cliffs at Etretat.

A swim
    in the rough foam
      of the sky

      would do you good,
        a stroll by the shoals.

You can wash grit
    from your countenance,

you can scour skeletal
    talc
    from your jeans.

The sea possesses a voice too.

You had to know that.

Consider your aberrance,
    it calls,

    how unlike the waves,

no shock of land can hold you.

How long
    until the Grecian door opens?

Some Norman woman,
    jagged   and lovely
    as the cliffs.

And as years
    pass, your children poach
    feathers from goslings,

take for themselves
    gods in white dresses.

Listen
    to the way they call curses
    on the icy chop.

Then one day,
    the boat stands are gone,

only a lemon
    rind, a map,
    the flotilla now black flies
    swarming a horizon.

What have you done
    lingering here?

You should have left long ago.

Musk thistle clamors
    over the path, and the stars
        are keyholes in the cloud mass.

Oh, to see the ruddy
faces
    of the daughters now!

But over the hill,
    you smell wild
        mustard and quack grass.

    You hear cries like a child's

like a loon's.

Self-Portrait at Twenty-Eight in Iberia

After Gauguin's Le Christ juane, *1889*

And when I dove into the water,
I was not me anymore.

I was salmon light
cast weary on the Turia,

incautious as Gauguin's brushstrokes.
I was his ferocity

as he rendered *fruchtshale
und zitronen* in Prussian blue.

You hate Gauguin. His brash
and selfish life.

What would you have made
of me then, Lydia?

My beard a breath of industrial smoke,
my life a tattered bag I shouldered.

I lived cruelly through winter.

How many flexes of muscle was I
from crushing an old man's wrist,

a pensioner riding home,
fearful for the open flap of my satchel.

The riptide
of my strength and anger

breaking in me even as he pulled away.
I bought my way to Valencia,

its water so clear and cobalt,
it could have been another sky.

You should have seen it.
The blue-lit ghost of sundown,

the glow of the city like the wheat
hillsides Gauguin brushed.

And couldn't forget the man's face
contorted into a pain I wanted,

wanted to goad that pain into song
like a guitarist hungering up a neck.

I watched the waves, relearning
gentleness. To the bag I said, *I will shred*

you like a flayed animal. To the river,
you are a spine the juane light kisses.

Poem with Sky Cradled in Shrunken Limbs

I woke to the black tree
Bill posted:

the honey locust's
three withered tusks
    piercing
        a blue aurora.

The ground was a slaughter floor

    its featureless white,
        frozen—

everything dead or asleep,

branchlets
    like dark capillaries
exploded
        on snow.

Hadn't I seen the image
    when I would drive
    the I-90 corridor,

coming down
    the incline
        to Rock Cut,
    Pierce Lake?

The year I was asked
    to leave
    the dorms,

year I slept
    in the backseat.

I'd forgotten it
    but retained
the incision of light
    through the windshield,

the not-sleeping.

Sleep debt
medical professionals call it,

the gap between the circadian

    clock
    and what the body needs

to wake.

To whom
    do I owe
        what?
I wondered.

To the hypothalamus
    erasing the images,
    which in waking
    become ghosts

        of another attention.

To my parents
    who mailed a box of cans

the year I locked arms
    with Marxists
    against a war we'd never see.

Feathers for mangled limbs.
    Flag-draped boxes
    for graves.

And didn't they carry love
    out of me,
    brick by brick

the year the snow-worn branches
    were snipers.

And in the dorms
    where I wasn't welcome
    a deflated god hummed
    every hymn he knew.

Year I boiled noodles
    in old china.

Year the microwave counted
    backward,
    hynopompic

        to insomnia.

First Course in Demonology

When you finally live alone,
even the curtain
printed with tube stops
will loom.

The tracks circle eerily—
Queensbury transfer
to Wembley only to link
to Mudchute, Queensbury again.

Don't be afraid.

At night count drafts
pulsing the vent,

then the morning
songs of mimids.

    ...

If you spy the *baberek*,
beat a spice platter.

If the specter huntsman
finds you, sing,
Bring us their hearts,

because ghouls starve
for admiration.

For everything there is
a rule—

grimoires and icons
you cannot cross,

edicts devils
dare not defy.

When summer spins out

in half-gestures,
let it—
the river's indifference,

her hands kneading,
passionate

and sure.

. . .

If I tell you the hands
hold no power, will you listen?

That the hands tell
the boldest lies.

Name what binds one body to another.

Not iron bands, not devil's
traps, brick dust,

even that pull
which attracts hands
to the heat of the back
where she'd inked birds
of paradise

bright as souls.

Think only briefly of how she
loved your digits
as you traced
crown and scapulae,

rounding curves like rosaries.
of how she gasped your name,

your common name.

August 5, 2012

On August 5th, 2012, white supremacist Wade Michael Page entered a Sikh temple in Oak Creek, Wisconsin. Wade killed six members of the temple before police were able to respond. In the gun battle that followed, Wade injured an officer before fatally shooting himself in the head.

There's a picture of me
    Traci took
        on the rocks
            in Whitefish Bay.

It looks like I'm walking on
    the ivory water
        past the darkest part
of the corona

settling
    on the gnash of waves.

The waves are muted
            and methodical
    like a child
    pushing a prayer

from his breath   to his palm.

I set the picture down.

Since the groundskeepers
reaped the field north of town,

I hear a din
    of cicadas, their thrum
        a subtle crack

in the silence my parents keep.

My job is to listen
    to the insects,
    to the gunfire

from the alley where boys

        stipple Sprite bottles.

    Stretchers
    pass
        on the news.

One policeman stops,
    takes off his helmet,

the other turns.

In the photo it looks like I
    want to step
        over the horizon with its last light

unfolding. But I would miss
    the babble of water,
        the yips
            of my dog racing across a field.

I don't know.

Do I want the strength to accept
   what Job had to,
      what God gives back—
           the new wife's soft hands,
             the children
           listening for the trample
           of their father's herd?

At night, they collect
   the lives
      of insects in jars.

They spread
   their bodies
      on the meadow,

laying their ears
           to the dirt.

Triptych with Burning Branches (Refrain)

After Hopper's Nighthawks, *1942*

I learned you wrong the summer
rains broke the levies' backs.

My father hung you in his office.
He knew your homage,

knew what shadow follows.
Unlike your original

a range of wrinkles
disfigured your stranger.

Hours alone, I'd stare
you down—

diner on one side,
vacant corner on the other.

...

Yes, years bleached
you to parchment.

In the gallery, I don't think
of your mannequin digits.

In the gallery, clouds
the color of turmeric peel

past skylight.
Strange now to find you—

my father's office
long another's, print

recycled and replaced.
You're the length of a lover's hip

I can't recall.
I wonder if I am

at home in this world,
in the known, yet unknown

diner, in this country of fire-
scripted trees.

Elegy for the Deodand

He couldn't remember the story—
how the bull elk
happened into his neighbors'

garden, what signal
warned them.

The neighbor and wife sheltered
in the bathroom when the elk

charged. The glass portico crashed
then a rain of sparkling

hornets, a god gashed
and bleating.

But no one transcends
the miracle of muscle and nerve,

not even the one
who believes he is chosen to.

What happened next
is what often happens:

the beast mewing
beside the loveseat,
lost in the world of his blood.

Then the shot like the crack of
a bone giving way beneath a boot.

Punished for what
he couldn't understand,

or is punishment
the word?

Deodand, I think,
that principle of law
where the rain-soaked bough

that crushed the ox driver's spine
must be splintered,

the waterwheel whose paddles
drowned the bather burned.

*A thing forfeited
or given to God*, the text says.

To believe this,
you must imagine the world

as two natures. One where bulls
lock antlers over harems.

The other a foreign code
under which the bull suffered.

Why the authority of one
over another, you might ask?

Glowering at his own posture,
could the creature think there is

one type of beauty we must break
through to find another?

That we might die
trying to reach it.

II.

Disciplining the Body

What emerged from the cellar
    of the abandoned summer house
was a fox cub,
           alive
    and mewing, though motherless.

It cried, muted, while we shot
    the Glock. And when Thom
threw open the hatch door,
    I wasn't thinking of the farm dog

which rushed down the stairs,
    throttled
        a blur of scarlet.

The cub's bones
    twisted, snapped,
not a significant noise,
    not what I'd expected.

Then it happened like this:

    we were quiet,
and you walked past
    the dogbane to where
the cub lay heaving,
    slipped the safety and fired.

Not solemnly,
    but suddenly steeled.

And after the recoil,
    you let that stiffness
slide off you

    as if the crack
echoing the fallow acre
    toward the silo,
its grain door
    rusty, eddying with the wind,

cracked you too.

The living
    leave their ghosts behind.

Later, we walked
    through the turnrows.
And later, Thom married Kayla.

The day of the rehearsal
    the wedding party
practiced *Thriller*
    in the church's basement.

Vine left, said Thom,
    now upper body rock,
cross step left.
    Thom said to watch you.

He restarted the song,
    and you shambled forward,
head ticking: one, five, seven.
    Your shoulders,
a yolk,
        bobbed

         in perfect phrase
to the double-beat of the chorus,

when Michael glides
      backwards
            on the soundstage
in what
      must have seemed

an impossibility,

      pure
muscular alchemy,

some unthinkable level
of control.

Self-Portrait of Daughter as Eurydice

Father wouldn't tear the barn down,
and now it hovers in the dark

conjuring murders.
In the wedding photos, he's monstrous.

He ripped miles of shingles
before fever, injury.

Strength stripped by the inexplicable,
but doesn't life demand

bargains with the inexplicable?
The reign of gravity

on this field, the sure, salty
push of wind.

Now mother spends summers
culling thicket grass

from spoonwoods,
spurning what breeds in the barn.

She has no strength left
to break.

At noon, she turns leaden water
to strands of gold.

I wouldn't watch
her sink, though I can endure

biting hot sand,
my heels brazen red.

But I am not your Helen. Father,
I am proud enough

prudent enough not to turn.

A Prayer for Anesthetics and Illusion

Pluck me from these prairie grasses,
    this armageddon
        of withered Dutch elms.

The ditches are painted
    with carcass and scorched oil.

The sunset's flush remnants
    enflame a farmhouse

and dissolve.

Tonight, I have so much
to say to you.

Tomorrow,
    surgeons will slice
my father's knee,

severing
    to reveal tendons
    in need of rewiring, pins.

I know material life
    is the illusion,
    the burden.

I know my onus is a stale hamburger,
    radio spinning to
    no station. Nothing for miles.

I count hours to the fireworks
    separating south from

blank canvas. To a needle.

    A sponge. My father's galaxy
        of fragile nerves.

Will you be the scalpel
    dividing the veil of skin?
    The germ?

Will you be the nerves
    stung to disconnection?

To retain the onus
    he needs no tenderness,

only nerves parlaying
      baffled language.

You have heard me
    in the abyss,
    the batter of my mallet hands
    on wheel.

You have sent me the green
      tongues of saints,

the muted rain on glass.

On Dignity

After Whistler's Nocturne in Black and Gold: The Falling Rocket, *1875*

These old Iowa farmhouses
throw glyphs of shadow across acres.

Wasn't it you who swore
to protest here till the war ended,

then never to fight again?
Pinned the red star

to a beret and watched
as light played havoc

on the thorny lot outside.
Didn't you measure the heft

of a brick in your hand
before you tested it

against your neighbor's window?
The window he iced

My Country, Love it or Leave it.
You replanted his garden

that summer and buried
the pin and pamphlets,

crisp and white as finger bones,
buried them and didn't wonder what grew.

Asters, posies,
the incendiary flowers of

Whistler's Falling Rocket,
its sparked minarets, gossamer

avalanches skulking mudflats—
you studied it in school,

the phantasmal jonquils blooming
beneath paint and canvas.

You could have traced the physical beauty
of that city reveled in incendiary spirals.

What was that beauty, you wondered
what were those marches to the man

who picked gnarled glass from
purpling tomatoes,

who you discovered kept
his son's dog tags on a hook in the shed.

Blighted October and the sky
soaking everything in half-light.

What use for beauty here?
you wondered. Just

the slow, sure strike of shovel
looking for what and how deep.

Self-Portrait of Rossetti Among the Dead

Elizabeth Siddal, wife of Dante Gabriel Rossetti, died of an overdose of laudanum in 1862. Rossetti painted her likeness over and over, including in his famous image of Dante's Beatrice. Two years after completing this work, Rossetti had a nervous breakdown and committed suicide.

The dead are still with us.
They finger lockets from

dressers. They sing
waltzes to the bells

shrieking in my head.
Imagine how it hurts:

to render the covert
of each cadmium wing.

Imagine a plum glade
guarded by murderers.

I will show you: here is my
beloved dressed as perdition's.

Bathe in her hair's immolation.
Let death eat from your palm.

At times, can't you hear it,
each susurration of your blood

like a mad horse throttling
his load toward hell?

Listen to the rain clopping
cobbles, toucan turning gyres.

The world is a tiny orb
tossed in this trembling.

Are you Virgil here to lead me?
Charon here to drown me?

I am Rossetti, painter of
the frocks of saints,

my love damned by laudanum,
me by chloral hydrate.

Because man must sleep,
and nothing does not suffer.

Give me harrowed lips.
Let me whiten the loaves of her fingers.

If you've come to offer me
viperous wind, viperous wind, I choose it.

Show me the squalling river
and take my rusty coins.

But I will ride in the mad
carriage of my own blood.

Burning and Getting Burnt

Exhaustion
overtook me in my dream.

And when I woke, it was still there.
A mild dark was dissipating
through the blinds.

The way it begins to burn
in rose or violet,
its uniformity,

tells me darkness
is one thing
and not a multitude.

I've seen wildfires
smoke away a sky in Utah—

I can't get any closer
to what happened.

This New Year's, I vowed not to work
for less than what a job is worth.

Then I never asked how much
the job paid

until the three hundred dollars
appeared. Still bedroom,

I am angry at you
every morning,

your dog sounds
and mellow warmth.

At what I must do
to keep you.

At the bathmat deadpan
in the shower.
Angry at the many faces

of darkness and the lilies
threatening to emerge.

Early in the season,
they must break
the weighty earth,

then crack the shell.
I want to be there
when they do.

I want to go back
to Utah where the river
empties its anger

over and over, rowing
against something,

toward something:
a splintered precipice, a shore.

Pentimento

After Tissot's Abraham and the Three Angels, *1902*

Abraham watches the men pass.

Or are they men at all?
    Mal'akim or messengers of a God
    so holy his name is a thousand bees.

In Tissot's vision, they're not winged,
    no weltering locks,
    no blood-rusted swords.

Their cream *thawbs* veil
    human features—
        thick eyebrows,
        old men's jaws.

One bevels his chin,
    his face worn.

How tired the messenger
    must be—opening
    his satchel of pestilence,

unsheathing the sky's fiery wrack.

Now they pass the field
        of brambled monk's pepper

like the roe deer
    emerging
        to eat morning's tender grass.

And Abraham
    who's cleaned his nails remains on the mesa.

And feels what as
God turns his *paniym*

to the aged shepherd
    to haggle slaughter?

No classical painter captured this.
Below the murderers went
        on with their grisly work.

And saw what?

An insane hermit
        hunched in his robe.

So different from the holy men,
    they must have thought,
        who cut open the children's bellies.

The sun nesting behind
    a vellum of hills,

its flicker fighting,
    chiaroscuro on the crags
        as in Caravaggio.

Caravaggio,
    thousands of years later, considers

the castrated boy,
        the lute player.

After the first layer,
    begins to trace
        with his handle
            image of a lute,
            image of a carafe,

then pauses,
            then changes his mind.

Soviet Film

Let the professor turn off the projector.
    Let the students file out.

A Spruce Grouse
    bellows from the maw of the river,

but this Wisconsin town

is disappeared,
    its conical mounds—
now Siberian slopes

        glazed
                cinereal.

Snow shining
    the color of starvation,
  intense enough to make a man

kill his friend.

You are there
    in the window
    watching them, some rubbing
palms,
    some bartering cigarettes.

One hums, one runs
    a nervous hand across a shoulder.

Where to go
    but back to the bunks?

What to speak to frostbitten stars
      pricking the sorority roof,
                      to fingers
         too famished to point?

Let the students ford ditches
          glutted with cadaverous

silver. You are busy.
     You are watching your visage
     in glass, backing up,

     like Vertov, you're an image
     recording an image, dredging

lakes of your pupils.

What dead you find there

you cannot save.

Self-Portrait as Hunters in the Snow

After Brueghel's Hunters in the Snow, *1565*

I was terrible at things,
of course. When the snow

came to cocoon, I was, for this
reason, rounding the school

track in tennis shorts.
A sky like Brueghel's,

a sea of muddy glass.
Coach counted my laps—

five per missed free throw.
He'd been rehired a month

after he'd been fired for
battering a ref with a chair.

The ref dragged his
left foot like a cripple,

coach told us,
a California faggot.

He sang the national anthem
as he drove us through frost-

stricken forests.
What were we doing

wandering woods where
elders say a man swore a pact

with the devil for a strong
horse, for a glass of brandy?

Brueghel's hunters
must have asked.

Those hunters, Bavarians,
saw the thickets bereft

of piebald does. Crossed
frozen tidewaters

of the Rhine,
jutting spires

of rock, dead furies
bursting the permafrost.

What but necessity
kept them trundling,

nearly dead among the dead?
What need kept me running?

*You have to master at least
one thing*, the coach said.

I understood how dawn
practices, his chair

he'd proudly hobbled
mastered him.

But how to explain what
weakness kept me?

How to understand
what a voice

echoing through the wood
needed to say,

but get up, son,
get up, walk away?

Dürer in the Valley of Oleanders

After Arco, *1495*

One wastes time
      loving anything

this much: the foliage
      won't still,

shuttering and trading
      shadows

in the coronary earth.
      The pigment

and sugar get it wrong, Agnes.
      Like my language

in the Venetian's mouth.
      To translate

tires me—oleanders to forks,
      cliffs to decapitated

generals. It's the errors; always
      the clumsy tool

in the clumsier hand. I am
      so much a man

before this makeshift easel. Agnes,
      on the outskirts

of Arco there is little to traffic.
        Laughter of women,

one muscling a wheelbarrow,
        others basketing

oranges: all indifferent as the cries
        of pelagic birds.

Don't fear when I tell you I love
        this monotony.

I'm coming home. Because
        what is this love

wasted on vineyards and watchtowers
        haunted by owls?

Down the Alps—a rumble
        of horned deer.

I swirl the pigment, add the tarred road.
        The deer grow louder.

I feel mad with the rush of it.
        A craftsman of hares.

Carver of blood-hungry steeds.
        Do not name me a god.

I am not. I am those animals,
        reckless and ragged.

Speak my name, and I will tear
        this mountain to your will.

Politics of the Afterlife

The wasp nest the drones built
    is finished,

and at night I hear them
    suckling nectar

and hemolymph from victims.

I strip the porch boards,
fumigate—

pyrethin,
    which scorches innards,
        rages like a house fire
before it kills.

They can all burn,
    I tell Thom.

Gehenna—a valley
    where the sacrificed are stacked,

where I ferry the nest
    after I've turned it
        to a grey tomb safe
        for children.

I want to be bigger.

Unconscionable life,
    where I must kill

more than I can save,
I want to love you. You

and Rob Bell,
    who wrote that Ghandi
        wasn't in hell.

A thousand parishioners
    left his church.

An article said people got uncomfortable
        with the idea others
    didn't have to suffer
when they should suffer, even if
        it's horribly, with extreme

instruments of torture for good.

We need a God
        capable of wrath

one Pastor wrote as if God
            were his echo.

The article doesn't indicate
    what the pastor did after this,

but I imagine him
    turning from presbytery
        to nave,

reluctantly
    into the spring
        where ferns and flowers

    the color of persimmons
            swatched the lawn.

And he thought
        how greedy the flowers
look, jockeying for an angle

    on unclouded sky.

Yes, and how survival

made them cruel
    at times.

Thick malaise coming,
    anvil clouds
        coaxed

into obscurity.

I have coveted,
    and I have been coolly vengeful, Lord.

But you are much larger,
    much kinder than me.

You can be like the clouds
   who when they rain
sound like wings
   beating and beating
the dark.

Three Trees for Lydia

After Rembrandt's The Three Trees, *1643*

Some believe the hill is Golgotha,

the trees
    two thieves and a God.

Then who are the fisherman and his wife?

Peasants who bowed
    to cairns and goby,
        idols
            of thrashing fish?

Or it's Saskia
    with Rembrandt,
        patiently awaiting

what's pulled
    from the riverine darkness.

I imagine husband and wife
    seated
        before kindling.

They're so small, Lydia,
    amidst the magnanimity
        of the flats,

the fingerprint sky smothered
    by steam.

As I turn the print, your hair
    hangs lithe as the lines
    of Rembrandt's échoppe.

A sliced lemon,
    almond light
        dapple the cutting board.

There are roses,
rain smoking
    from the forest.

But not one of the maples
    resembles a cross.
        No messiahs,
        no thieves,

just what asks
    to be stolen, what demands.

Acknowledgments

AGNI: "Self-Portrait at Twenty-Eight in Iberia" and "Pentimento"

Alaska Quarterly Review: "Portrait of Vincent in Nuenen" and "A Prayer for Anesthetics and Illusion"

Blackbird: "Elegy for the Deodand," "Disciplining the Body" and "Politics of the Afterlife."

Colorado Review: "Tryptich with Burning Branches (Refrain)"

Cream City Review: "August 5, 2012"

Harvard Review: "Tryptich for Nighthawks"

Michigan Quarterly Review: "How to Fall in Love with the Prairie"

Mid-American Review: "Self-Portrait of Rossetti Among the Dead"

Ninth Letter: "Soviet Film"

Pleiades: "Aubade for the World in Miniature"

Rhino: "Three Trees for Lydia"

Sugar House Review: "First Course in Demonology" and "Burning and Getting Burnt"

Verse Daily: "Dürer in the Valley of Oleanders"

Waxwing: "Lesser Evil" and "Gentle"

West Branch: "Poem with Sky Cradled in Shrunken Limbs" and "Dürer in the Valley of Oleanders"

About the Author

Kyle McCord is the author of five books of poetry including *You Are Indeed an Elk, But This is Not the Forest You Were Born to Graze* (Gold Wake, 2015), and *Gentle, World, Gentler*, from Ampersand Books. His work has been featured in *AGNI, Boston Review, Harvard Review, Ploughshares, TriQuarterly* and elsewhere. Kyle has received grants from the Academy of American Poets, the Vermont Studio Center, and the Baltic Writing Residency. The founding editor of *American Microreviews and Interviews*, he recently completed his Ph.D. at University of North Texas, now lives in Des Moines, Iowa, and teaches at Drake University.

About the Book

Magpies in the Valley of Oleanders was designed at Trio House Press through the collaboration of:

Matt Mauch, Lead Editor
the-athenaeum.org, Cover Photo: File Source
"View of the Arco Valley in the Tyrol",
Albrecht Dürer, ca. 1495 (PD), Cover Art
Dorinda Wegener, Cover Design
Lea Deschenes, Interior Design

The text is set in Adobe Caslon Pro.

The publication of this book is made possible, whole or in part, by the generous support of the following individuals and/or agencies:

Anonymous

About the Press

Trio House Press is a collective press. Individuals within our organization come together and are motivated by the primary shared goal of publishing distinct American voices in poetry. All THP published poets must agree to serve as Collective Members of the Trio House Press for twenty-four months after publication in order to assist with the press and bring more Trio books into print. Award winners and published poets must serve on one of four committees: Production and Design, Distribution and Sales, Educational Development, or Fundraising and Marketing. Our Collective Members reside in cities from New York to San Francisco.

Trio House Press adheres to and supports all ethical standards and guidelines outlined by the CLMP.

Trio House Press, Inc. is dedicated to the promotion of poetry as literary art, which enhances the human experience and its culture. We contribute in an innovative and distinct way to American Poetry by publishing emerging and established poets, providing educational materials, and fostering the artistic process of writing poetry. For further information, or to consider making a donation to Trio House Press, please visit us online at: www.triohousepress.org.

Other Trio House Press Books you might enjoy:

Bone Music by Stephen Cramer
    2015 Louise Bogan Award selected by Kimiko Hahn

Rigging a Chevy into a Time Machine and Other Ways to Escape a Plague by Carolyn Hembree
    2015 Trio Award Winner selected by Neil Shepard

Your Immaculate Heart by Annmarie O'Connell, 2015

The Alchemy of My Mortal Form by Sandy Longhorn
    2014 Louise Bogan Winner selected by Carol Frost

What the Night Numbered by Bradford Tice
    2014 Trio Award Winner selected by Peter Campion

Flight of August by Lawrence Eby
    2013 Louise Bogan Winner selected by Joan Houlihan

The Consolations by John W. Evans
    2013 Trio Award Winner selected by Mihaela Moscaliuc

Fellow Odd Fellow by Steven Riel, 2013

Clay by David Groff
    2012 Louise Bogan Winner selected by Michael Waters

Gold Passage by Iris Jamahl Dunkle
    2012 Trio Award Winner selected by Ross Gay

If You're Lucky Is a Theory of Mine by Matt Mauch, 2012

www.ingramcontent.com/pod-product-compliance
Lightning Source LLC
Chambersburg PA
CBHW020622300426
44113CB00007B/753